Earthquakes and Tsunamis

By Mary Draper

Contents

Introduction

An earthquake makes the ground shake and crack. It starts a long way under the surface of Earth.

An earthquake can be very dangerous. People are sometimes hurt or killed. They can lose their homes, and be left with no food or water.

People cannot stop an earthquake from happening, but scientists are learning about where and when an earthquake might happen.

A tsunami is a very large and powerful wave. When an earthquake happens under the ocean, it can make a tsunami.

old Japanese print of a tsunami

A tsunami can be very high by the time it hits the land, and people often have no warning.

tsunami damage

What Is an Earthquake?

The plates in Earth's crust are moving very slowly all the time. The place where two plates meet is called a fault.

Sometimes the plates get stuck when they move along a fault. The two plates keep pushing until one side breaks, then there is a jerk and a shake. This is an earthquake.

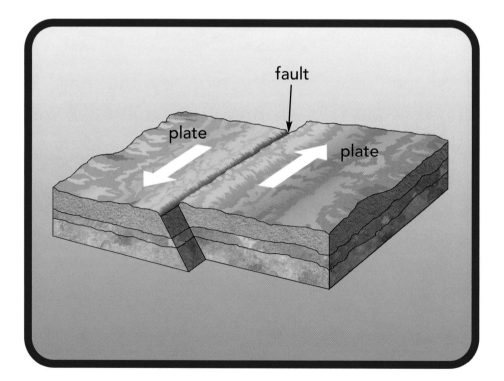

fault

plate

plate

Shock Waves

The place where the earthquake reaches the surface of Earth is called the epicenter.

Shock waves fan out from the epicenter in all directions and make the ground shake.

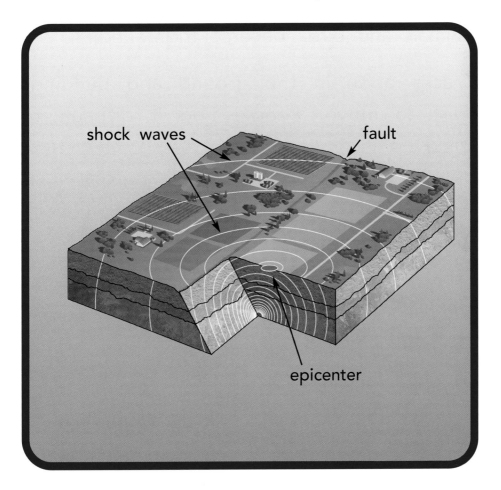

shock waves

fault

epicenter

When an Earthquake Happens

An earthquake starts with a rumbling sound, and people may feel the ground shaking slightly. These are the first shock waves.

Animals and birds become frightened.

Cracks open in the ground and buildings start to move. People find it difficult to stand up.

The last shock waves are usually the most dangerous, even at great distances. Buildings collapse, and landslides and rock falls start. The ground moves in "waves" and water comes up to the surface.

DID YOU KNOW?

An earthquake usually lasts for less than one minute.

Measuring Earthquakes

A special machine measures the shock waves during an earthquake. Scientists mark the shock waves on the Richter scale to tell us the size of an earthquake.

An earthquake that measures one or two on the Richter scale is not very strong, and people will not feel it. If an earthquake measures seven or more on the Richter scale, it will cause a lot of damage and many people could die.

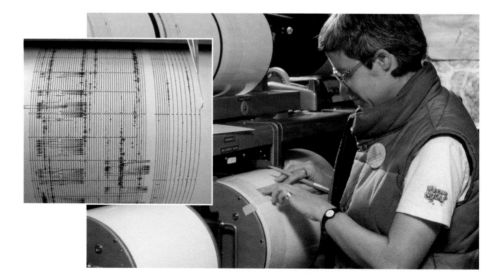

Nearly 2,000 years ago, the Chinese used a machine for sensing earthquakes. When an earthquake happened, a ball was shaken out of the mouth of one of the dragons. The ball fell into the mouth of one of the toads.

Earthquakes Around the World

The red dots on this map show us where big earthquakes have happened. The white lines show us the fault lines.

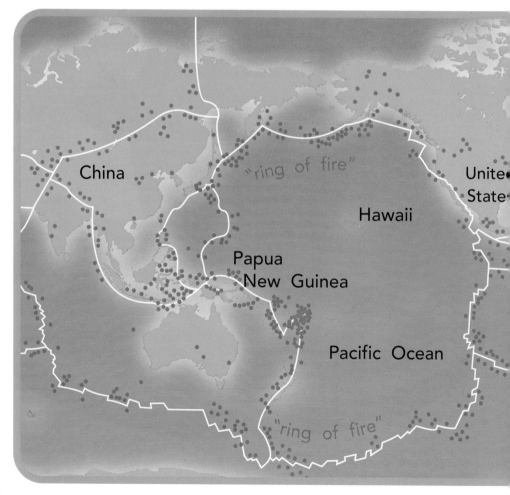

China

"ring of fire"

United States

Hawaii

Papua New Guinea

Pacific Ocean

"ring of fire"

Scientists call the edge of the Pacific Ocean the "ring of fire," because many earthquakes and volcanoes happen there.

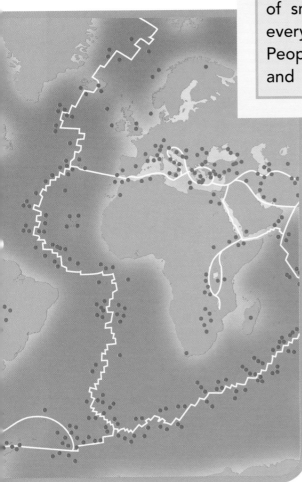

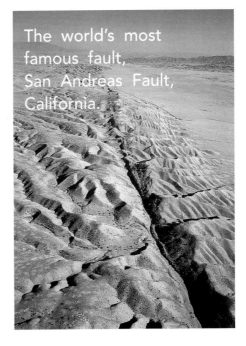

The world's most famous fault, San Andreas Fault, California.

Earthquake Damage

Some earthquakes cause no damage. Others do terrible damage to buildings and roads. People can be hurt or killed.

This man was rescued after an earthquake.

A big earthquake loosens rocks and soil. The soil slides down the sides of hills and mountains and makes a landslide. Sometimes whole towns are covered by landslides.

During an earthquake, gas and water pipes can be broken. Leaking gas can cause fires. The fires sometimes destroy buildings that didn't fall in the earthquake.

Broken water pipes and cracked wells make the water dirty. People who drink dirty water become sick.

Rescue Efforts

When an earthquake does a lot of damage, teams of rescuers come from other countries to help. They dig people out from under fallen buildings.

DID YOU KNOW?

Special dogs are used to help find people after a bad earthquake.

The rescuers give blankets, tents, and food to people who have lost their homes.

What Is a Tsunami?

When an earthquake happens under water, the shock waves make the water move in big, strong waves. The waves spread out from the epicenter and travel over long distances.

Near the coast the waves slow down and form into one huge wave. This is called a tsunami.

DID YOU KNOW?

A tsunami can travel almost as fast as a jet plane.

tsunami

shock waves

If an earthquake makes a landslide into the sea, the force of the land pushes the water away. The water then builds up into a tsunami.

landslide

Sometimes a volcanic eruption under the sea can cause a tsunami.

Tsunami Damage

When a tsunami hits the land, it can cause terrible damage, and people can be swept away by the water. A tsunami cannot be stopped. Because scientists do not know when a tsunami will happen, it is difficult for them to warn people.

Cities and towns can be destroyed by the power of the water.

tsunami damage, Hawaii

DID YOU KNOW?

Nearly three-quarters of all tsunamis in the world happen in the Pacific Ocean.

Tsunami Disaster

Papua New Guinea

Yesterday, there was an earthquake in the Pacific Ocean. A huge tsunami formed, which rolled across the ocean and hit some islands late last night. There was no time to warn the people along the coast. Thousands of people were drowned when the wave hit their houses by the sea.

Keeping People Safe

Today, scientists from around the world work together. They share information with each other, so that they can learn more about earthquakes and tsunamis. They still cannot say when an earthquake or tsunami might come, but there are other ways to help keep people safe.

Some buildings have been made in special ways, so that they will not fall down during an earthquake. These buildings have steel frames that will bend, rather than break.

This building has rubber in its foundations.

Questions

1. How long does an earthquake usually last?
2. How many earthquakes does Earth have every year that no one feels?
3. What can special dogs do after an earthquake?
4. How fast can a tsunami travel?
5. Where do most tsunamis happen?
6. Why are some buildings built on rubber?

Glossary

collapse	to fall down
epicenter	the place where the earthquake reaches Earth's surface
fault	where one plate meets another plate
jolt	a sudden move or shake
plates	the giant pieces that make up Earth's crust
Richter scale	a scale from one to ten that describes the size of an earthquake
shock waves	movement of the ground that spreads out from the earthquake's epicenter